CW00926254

Contents

21st Century – page 2

Transfers I – page 6

First Goals I – page 10

Red Cards – page 12

Memorable Goals – page 15

Memorable Games – page 18

Transfers II – page 21

Cup Games – page 24

First Goals II – page 27

21st Century answers – page 30

Transfers I answers – page 35

First Goals I answers – page 40

Red Cards answers – page 42

Memorable Goals answers – page 46

Memorable Games answers – page 50

Transfers II answers – page 53

Cup Games answers – page 57

First Goals II answers – page 61

21st Century

1) Who scored Aston Villa's first goal of the 21st Century?

2) Who was Aston Villa manager at the beginning of the 21st Century?

3) Who did David O'Leary replace as Aston Villa manager in 2003?

4) Roberto Di Matteo was Aston Villa manager for 12 games in 2016, how many of those games did he win?

5) Who was the clubs top goal scorer in the Championship in the 2016/17 season?

6) What squad number had Tyrone Mings worn since joining Aston Villa?

7) Against which team did Jack Grealish make his Aston Villa debut?

8) Who became the first Turkish player to represent Aston Villa when he signed in the year 2000?

9) Who became the clubs youngest ever goal scorer when he netted against MSK Zilina in the UEFA Cup in December 2008?

10) Which future Villa player lined up against them in the 2018 Play-Off Final for Fulham?

11) How many points did the team win during the relegation season of 2015/16?

12) Who took the throw-in which lead to Peter Enckelman's infamous own goal against Birmingham City in September 2002?

13) In what year did Randy Lerner complete his takeover of the club?

14) Who scored a hat-trick in the 4-0 away win over Middlesbrough in February 2006?

15) Villa lost 6-0 away at Newcastle in August 2010 after which Aston Villa player had missed a penalty with the score at 0-0?

16) Who became Aston Villa club captain following their relegation in 2016?

17) 2007 saw which two teams compete in the last ever FA Cup Semi-Final to be staged at Villa Park and what was the score?

18) Which two Aston Villa players won the PFA Young Player of the Year award for the 2008/09 and then 2009/10 seasons?

19) Which Villa player scored four times in the remarkable 5-5 draw with Nottingham Forest in November 2018?

20) Who put Villa 1-0 up away against Spurs in their first game back in the Premier League in August 2019 before the succumbed to a 3-1 loss late on?

Transfers I

1) Who did Stan Collymore sign for after leaving Villa in the year 2000?

2) From which club was Alpay bought in July 2000?

3) Which striker arrived from River Plate in January 2001?

4) Which utility player was sold to Everton in July 2000?

5) Goalkeeper Peter Schmeichel arrived on a free transfer from which club in July 2001?

6) From which club was Peter Crouch bought in March 2002?

7) Which defender was sold to Middlesbrough in July 2001?

8) Ulises De La Cruz was signed from which Scottish club in July 2002?

9) Which central midfielder arrived from Charlton in August 2002?

10) Who did Ian Taylor sign for after leaving Aston Villa in June 2003?

11) Which two players were purchased from Sunderland in the summer of 2003?

12) From which Italian club did Aston Villa buy Martin Laursen in May 2004?

13) Which goalkeeper was sold to Blackburn Rovers in January 2004?

14) Aston Villa bought which player from Manchester United in January 2005?

15) Striker Kevin Phillips was bought from where in June 2005?

16) Which club was Darius Vassell sold to in July 2005?

17) Villa bought which two players from Celtic in the summer of 2006?

18) From which club was Shaun Maloney bought in January 2007?

19) Who did Juan Pablo Angel sign for after leaving Aston Villa in April 2007?

20) Which centre back arrived from Fulham in August 2007?

21) Lee Hendrie left Aston Villa and signed on a free for which club in July 2007?

22) Which central midfielder was purchased from Chelsea in July 2008?

23) Who did Olof Mellberg sign for after leaving Villa in August 2008?

24) From which team was Fabian Delph signed in August 2009?

First Goals I

1) Gabby Agbonlahor

2) Juan Pablo Angel

3) Ashley Young

4) James Milner

5) Peter Crouch

6) Olof Mellberg

7) Nolberto Solano

8) Luke Moore

9) John Carew

10) Marlon Harewood

11) Emile Heskey

12) Thomas Hitzlsperger

13) Lee Hendrie

14) Gary Cahill

Red Cards

1) Dion Dublin was shown a straight red card for head-butting which Birmingham City player in March 2003?

2) Who was sent off in the 1-0 defeat to Crystal Palace in August 2019?

3) David Ginola was dismissed for lashing out at which Leicester City player in a 2-0 defeat at Villa Park in December 2001?

4) Which two Villa players were sent off in the 4-1 home defeat to Manchester United in October 2007?

5) Which goalkeeper was sent off against Southampton in October 2002?

6) Gabby Agbonlahor was harshly shown a red card for a challenge of which former Villa player in the 1-1 draw with Manchester United in December 2014?

7) Aston Villa lost 2-1 away to Charlton in December 2006, but which Villa player scored but was then dismissed later on in the match?

8) Which goalkeeper was sent off against Liverpool in March 2009, only for his red card to later be rescinded?

9) Who was sent off late on in the 1-0 win over Bolton in the Championship in September 2017?

10) Who was sent off in Tim Sherwood's first game as manager, the 2-1 defeat to Stoke City in February 2015?

11) Aston Villa came from behind to beat Sunderland 2-1 in January 2009 despite having which player dismissed?

12) Which midfielder was sent off in the Championship against Middlesbrough in September 2017?

13) Villa slipped to a 2-1 defeat against Spurs in November 2014 after which striker was sent off for slapping Ryan Mason?

14) Who was sent off for a first half elbow on West Ham's Aaron Cresswell in the 2-0 defeat in February 2016?

15) Villa managed to beat Rotherham 2-1 in April 2019 despite which defender being shown a straight red for handball?

Memorable Goals

1) Gary Cahill scored an acrobatic volley against Birmingham in April 2006, but what was the final score of the game?

2) Which unlikely player scored with a brilliant solo run against Birmingham in November 2018 to seal the 4-2 victory?

3) Who scored the winner in the 3-2 away win at Wolves in January 2012 with a shot from the edge of the area which crashed in off the underside of the bar?

4) John McGinn scored a sensational long-range volley against which team in September 2018?

5) Benito Carbone scored with a long-range curling effort to catch out the goalkeeper as Villa beat which team 3-2 in the FA Cup Fourth Round in 2000?

6) Paul Merson hit a powerful effort from the edge of the box to claim a 3-2 win on the last day of the season to relegate their opponents, who were they?

7) Gareth Barry cut inside off the left wing, beating two players, before curling a shot into the far corner with his right foot against which opposition in October 2006?

8) Which unlikely player hit a half volley on the turn to equalise in the 2-2 draw at Wigan in May 2013?

9) John Carew hit an outrageous first time volley from the edge of the box to lob the keeper in Villa's 2-2 draw with which side in March 2009?

10) Who scored with an unbelievable chest and volley from 30 yards out to help Villa on their win to a 3-1 win at Stoke in April 2013?

11) Stiliyan Petrov scored his incredible long-range goal against Derby County in April 2008, but which goalkeeper did he scored past?

12) Who provided the back-heeled assist for Andreas Weimann to score in the 3-1 victory at Anfield in December 2012?

13) Thomas Hitzlsperger scored with a scorching volley after flicking the ball up for himself on the edge of the box against which team in February 2005?

14) In April 2019 Villa played away at Leeds in a controversial encounter in which the home side scored, despite initially appearing to stop the game for an injury to Jonathan Kodija. Leeds then sportingly allowed which Villa player to score almost unchallenged from the kick off?

Memorable Games

1) Which two players scored for Aston Villa as they won the 2019 Championship Play-Off Final 2-1 over Derby County?

2) Which team did Villa beat 6-0 away from home in the Premier League in April 2008?

3) Who was in goal for Aston Villa as they lost 8-0 to Chelsea in December 2012?

4) Who scored the only goal as Villa won 1-0 at St Andrew's in March 2019?

5) Which team did Aston Villa beat 5-0 away from home in January 2004?

6) Which side won 6-0 at Villa Park in the Premier League in February 2016?

7) Aston Villa travelled to White Hart Lane as Spurs celebrated their 125th anniversary, but what was the score in the remarkable encounter?

8) Who scored a hat-trick as Villa came from 2-0 down to beat Spurs 4-2 away from home in April 2000?

9) What was the final score as Villa hammered Birmingham in the derby match of April 2008?

10) West Brom were beaten 2-1 at Villa Park in March 2015 thanks to a last minute penalty from who?

11) Aston Villa produced a surprise result to win 3-1 away from home on the opening day of the 2013/14 season against which team?

12) Villa won 1-0 at Old Trafford in December 2009, who scored the only goal of the game?

13) Who scored deep into second half stoppage time to claim a 2-1 victory over Watford in January 2020?

Transfers II

1) Who was Craig Gardner sold to in January 2010?

2) Which player was brought in from Lyon in January 2011?

3) From which club did full back Alan Hutton arrive in August 2011?

4) Who was Stewart Downing sold to in July 2011?

5) Ron Vlaar was bought from where in August 2012?

6) From which club did Aston Villa buy Christian Benteke in August 2012?

7) Which player arrived from Sevilla in the summer of 2013?

8) Which midfielder signed for Leicester City after leaving Villa in May 2014?

9) Which centre back arrived from Valencia in July 2014?

10) Which two forwards signed for Derby after leaving the club in June 2015?

11) Which goalkeeper arrived on a free transfer from Norwich in July 2015?

12) Which winger was bought from Barcelona in August 2015?

13) Who did Joe Cole sign for after leaving Aston Villa in January 2016?

14) Which Nottingham Forest midfield player was bought in January 2017?

15) Which central midfielder was sold to Everton in August 2016?

16) Defender Christopher Samba signed on a free from where in July 2017?

17) Which two players were sold to
Fiorentina in the summer of 2017?

18) From where was John McGinn signed in
August 2018?

19) Who was bought from Club Brugge in
June 2019?

20) Which player left to join Deportivo in
July 2018?

21) Which defender was bought from
Southampton in July 2019?

22) Who was brought in from Manchester
City in July 2019?

23) Which player was purchased from Genk
in the 2020 January transfer window?

24) From which Italian club was Pepe Reina
loaned in January 2020?

Cup Games

1) Who scored the only goal of the game as Chelsea beat Aston Villa 1-0 in the FA Cup Final in 2000?

2) Which club knocked Villa out in the Europa League Qualifying Rounds in both 2009 and 2010?

3) Who put Villa 1-0 up in the 2010 League Cup Final, before they eventually lost 2-1 to Manchester United?

4) Which Manchester United player controversially avoided a red card for his foul on Gabby Agbonlahor inside the first 5 minutes of that final?

5) Villa beat Ajax 2-1 in the Group Stage of the UEFA Cup in 2008 thanks to goal from which two players?

6) Aston Villa were knocked out of the League Cup in the Second Round in 2018 by which side?

7) Which team did Villa beat 8-3 away from home in the League Cup Second Round in 2005?

8) Which Croatian team knocked Aston Villa out of the UEFA Cup in the First Round in 2001?

9) Who scored the winner in the last minute of extra time to secure a 3-2 win over Leicester City in the League Cup Third Round in October 2006?

10) Who knocked Villa out of the FA Cup at the Third Round stage in 2018?

11) Villa reached the League Cup Final by beating Blackburn Rovers in the Semi Final Stage in 2010, but what was the remarkable score in the second leg?

12) Who scored the winner as Aston Villa beat Liverpool 2-1 in the 2015 FA Cup Semi Final?

13) What was the final score as Arsenal beat Villa in the 2015 FA Cup Final?

14) Which lower league team beat Villa over two legs in the 2013 League Cup Semi Final?

15) Who scored the Aston Villa goal as they lost the 2020 League Cup Final 2-1 to Manchester City?

First Goals II

1) Stiliyan Petrov

2) Christian Benteke

3) Milan Baros

4) Mbwana Samatta

5) Kevin Phillips

6) Darren Bent

7) Barry Bannan

8) Ciaran Clark

9) Rudy Gestede

10) Lewis Grabban

11) John Terry

12) Jack Grealish

13) John McGinn

14) Tyrone Mings

Answers

21st Century – Answers

1) Who scored Aston Villa's first goal of the 21st Century?
Gareth Southgate in a 2-1 win at Leeds

2) Who was Aston Villa manager at the beginning of the 21st Century?
John Gregory

3) Who did David O'Leary replace as Aston Villa manager in 2003?
Graham Taylor

4) Roberto Di Matteo was Aston Villa manager for 12 games in 2016, how many of those games did he win?
One – against Rotherham

5) Who was the clubs top goal scorer in the Championship in the 2016/17 season?
Jonathan Kodija

6) What squad number had Tyrone Mings worn since joining Aston Villa?

40

7) Against which team did Jack Grealish make his Aston Villa debut?

Manchester City

8) Who became the first Turkish player to represent Aston Villa when he signed in the year 2000?

Alpay

9) Who became the clubs youngest ever goal scorer when he netted against MSK Zilina in the UEFA Cup in December 2008?

Nathan Delfouneso

10) Which future Villa player lined up against them in the 2018 Play-Off Final for Fulham?

Matt Targett

11) How many points did the team win during the relegation season of 2015/16?

17

12) Who took the throw-in which lead to Peter Enckelman's infamous own goal against Birmingham City in September 2002?

Olof Mellberg

13) In what year did Randy Lerner complete his takeover of the club?

2006

14) Who scored a hat-trick in the 4-0 away win over Middlesbrough in February 2006?

Luke Moore

15) Villa lost 6-0 away at Newcastle in August 2010 after which Aston Villa player had missed a penalty with the score at 0-0?

John Carew

16) Who became Aston Villa club captain following their relegation in 2016?
Tommy Elphick

17) 2007 saw which two teams compete in the last ever FA Cup Semi-Final to be staged at Villa Park and what was the score?
Manchester United 4-1 Watford

18) Which two Aston Villa players won the PFA Young Player of the Year award for the 2008/09 and then 2009/10 seasons?
Ashley Young in 2008/09 and James Milner in 2009/10

19) Which Villa player scored four times in the remarkable 5-5 draw with Nottingham Forest in November 2018?
Tammy Abraham

20) Who put Villa 1-0 up away against Spurs in their first game back in the Premier League in August 2019 before the succumbed to a 3-1 loss late on?
John McGinn

Transfers I – Answers

1) Who did Stan Collymore sign for after leaving Villa in the year 2000?
Leicester City

2) From which club was Alpay bought in July 2000?
Fenerbahce

3) Which striker arrived from River Plate in January 2001?
Juan Pablo Angel

4) Which utility player was sold to Everton in July 2000?
Steve Watson

5) Goalkeeper Peter Schmeichel arrived on a free transfer from which club in July 2001?
Sporting Lisbon

6) From which club was Peter Crouch bought in March 2002?
Portsmouth

7) Which defender was sold to Middlesbrough in July 2001?
Gareth Southgate

8) Ulises De La Cruz was signed from which Scottish club in July 2002?
Hibernian

9) Which central midfielder arrived from Charlton in August 2002?
Mark Kinsella

10) Who did Ian Taylor sign for after leaving Aston Villa in June 2003?
Derby County

11) Which two players were purchased from Sunderland in the summer of 2003?
Gavin McCann and Thomas Sorensen

12) From which Italian club did Aston Villa buy Martin Laursen in May 2004?
AC Milan

13) Which goalkeeper was sold to Blackburn Rovers in January 2004?
Peter Enckelman

14) Aston Villa bought which player from Manchester United in January 2005?
Eric Djemba-Djemba

15) Striker Kevin Phillips was bought from where in June 2005?
Southampton

16) Which club was Darius Vassell sold to in July 2005?
Manchester City

17) Villa bought which two players from Celtic in the summer of 2006?
Stiliyan Petrov and Didier Agathe

18) From which club was Shaun Maloney bought in January 2007?
Celtic

19) Who did Juan Pablo Angel sign for after leaving Aston Villa in April 2007?
New York Red Bulls

20) Which centre back arrived from Fulham in August 2007?
Zat Knight

21) Lee Hendrie left Aston Villa and signed on a free for which club in July 2007?
Sheffield United

22) Which central midfielder was purchased from Chelsea in July 2008?
Steve Sidwell

23) Who did Olof Mellberg sign for after leaving Villa in August 2008?
Juventus

24) From which team was Fabian Delph
signed in August 2009?
Leeds United

First Goals I – Answers

1) Gabby Agbonlahor
   Everton

2) Juan Pablo Angel
   Coventry City

3) Ashley Young
   Newcastle United

4) James Milner
   Tottenham Hotspur

5) Peter Crouch
   Newcastle United

6) Olof Mellberg
   Manchester United

7) Nolberto Solano
   Fulham

8) Luke Moore
   Middlesbrough

9) John Carew
   West Ham United

10) Marlon Harewood
    Wrexham

11) Emile Heskey
    Portsmouth

12) Thomas Hitzlsperger
    Leicester City

13) Lee Hendrie
    Coventry City

14) Gary Cahill
    Birmingham City

Red Cards – Answers

1) Dion Dublin was shown a straight red card for head-butting which Birmingham City player in March 2003?
Robbie Savage

2) Who was sent off in the 1-0 defeat to Crystal Palace in August 2019?
Trezeguet

3) David Ginola was dismissed for lashing out at which Leicester City player in a 2-0 defeat at Villa Park in December 2001?
Dennis Wise

4) Which two Villa players were sent off in the 4-1 home defeat to Manchester United in October 2007?
Nigel Reo-Coker and Scott Carson

5) Which goalkeeper was sent off against Southampton in October 2002?
Peter Enckelman

6) Gabby Agbonlahor was harshly shown a red card for a challenge of which former Villa player in the 1-1 draw with Manchester United in December 2014?
Ashley Young

7) Aston Villa lost 2-1 away to Charlton in December 2006, but which Villa player scored but was then dismissed later on in the match?
Gareth Barry

8) Which goalkeeper was sent off against Liverpool in March 2009, only for his red card to later be rescinded?
Brad Friedel

9) Who was sent off late on in the 1-0 win over Bolton in the Championship in September 2017?
Neil Taylor

10) Who was sent off in Tim Sherwood's first game as manager, the 2-1 defeat to Stoke City in February 2015?
Ron Vlaar

11) Aston Villa came from behind to beat Sunderland 2-1 in January 2009 despite having which player dismissed?
Ashley Young

12) Which midfielder was sent off in the Championship against Middlesbrough in September 2017?
Henri Lansbury

13) Villa slipped to a 2-1 defeat against Spurs in November 2014 after which striker was sent off for slapping Ryan Mason?
Christian Benteke

14) Who was sent off for a first half elbow on West Ham's Aaron Cresswell in the 2-0 defeat in February 2016?
Jordan Ayew

15) Villa managed to beat Rotherham 2-1 in April 2019 despite which defender being shown a straight red for handball?
Tyrone Mings

Memorable Goals – Answers

1) Gary Cahill scored an acrobatic volley against Birmingham in April 2006, but what was the final score of the game?
Aston Villa 3-1 Birmingham City

2) Which unlikely player scored with a brilliant solo run against Birmingham in November 2018 to seal the 4-2 victory?
Alan Hutton

3) Who scored the winner in the 3-2 away win at Wolves in January 2012 with a shot from the edge of the area which crashed in off the underside of the bar?
Robbie Keane

4) John McGinn scored a sensational long-range volley against which team in September 2018?
Sheffield Wednesday

5) Benito Carbone scored with a long-range curling effort to catch out the goalkeeper as Villa beat which team 3-2 in the FA Cup Fourth Round in 2000?
Leeds United

6) Paul Merson hit a powerful effort from the edge of the box to claim a 3-2 win on the last day of the season to relegate their opponents, who were they?
Coventry City

7) Gareth Barry cut inside off the left wing, beating two players, before curling a shot into the far corner with his right foot against which opposition in October 2006?
Tottenham Hotspur

8) Which unlikely player hit a half volley on the turn to equalise in the 2-2 draw at Wigan in May 2013?
Ron Vlaar

9) John Carew hit an outrageous first time volley from the edge of the box to lob the keeper in Villa's 2-2 draw with which side in March 2009?
Stoke City

10) Who scored with an unbelievable chest and volley from 30 yards out to help Villa on their win to a 3-1 win at Stoke in April 2013?
Matt Lowton

11) Stiliyan Petrov scored his incredible long-range goal against Derby County in April 2008, but which goalkeeper did he scored past?
Roy Carroll

12) Who provided the back-heeled assist for Andreas Weimann to score in the 3-1 victory at Anfield in December 2012?
Christian Benteke

13) Thomas Hitzlsperger scored with a scorching volley after flicking the ball up for himself on the edge of the box against which team in February 2005?
Portsmouth

14) In April 2019 Villa played away at Leeds in a controversial encounter in which the home side scored, despite initially appearing to stop the game for an injury to Jonathan Kodija. Leeds then sportingly allowed which Villa player to score almost unchallenged from the kick off?
Albert Adomah

Memorable Games – Answers

1) Which two players scored for Aston Villa as they won the 2019 Championship Play-Off Final 2-1 over Derby County?
Anwar El Ghazi and John McGinn

2) Which team did Villa beat 6-0 away from home in the Premier League in April 2008?
Derby County

3) Who was in goal for Aston Villa as they lost 8-0 to Chelsea in December 2012?
Brad Guzan

4) Who scored the only goal as Villa won 1-0 at St Andrew's in March 2019?
Jack Grealish

5) Which team did Aston Villa beat 5-0 away from home in January 2004?
Leicester City

6) Which side won 6-0 at Villa Park in the Premier League in February 2016?
Liverpool

7) Aston Villa travelled to White Hart Lane as Spurs celebrated their 125th anniversary, but what was the score in the remarkable encounter?
4-4

8) Who scored a hat-trick as Villa came from 2-0 down to beat Spurs 4-2 away from home in April 2000?
Dion Dublin

9) What was the final score as Villa hammered Birmingham in the derby match of April 2008?
5-1

10) West Brom were beaten 2-1 at Villa Park in March 2015 thanks to a last minute penalty from who?
Christian Benteke

11) Aston Villa produced a surprise result to win 3-1 away from home on the opening day of the 2013/14 season against which team?
Arsenal

12) Villa won 1-0 at Old Trafford in December 2009, who scored the only goal of the game?
Gabby Agbonlahor

13) Who scored deep into second half stoppage time to claim a 2-1 victory over Watford in January 2020?
Tyrone Mings

Transfers II – Answers

1) Who was Craig Gardner sold to in January 2010?
Birmingham City

2) Which player was brought in from Lyon in January 2011?
Jean Makoun

3) From which club did full back Alan Hutton arrive in August 2011?
Tottenham Hotspur

4) Who was Stewart Downing sold to in July 2011?
Liverpool

5) Ron Vlaar was bought from where in August 2012?
Feyenoord

6) From which club did Aston Villa buy Christian Benteke in August 2012?
Genk

7) Which player arrived from Sevilla in the summer of 2013?
Antonio Luna

8) Which midfielder signed for Leicester City after leaving Villa in May 2014?
Marc Albrighton

9) Which centre back arrived from Valencia in July 2014?
Philippe Senderos

10) Which two forwards signed for Derby after leaving the club in June 2015?
Darren Bent and Andreas Weimann

11) Which goalkeeper arrived on a free transfer from Norwich in July 2015?
Mark Bunn

12) Which winger was bought from Barcelona in August 2015?
Adama Traore

13) Who did Joe Cole sign for after leaving Aston Villa in January 2016?
Coventry City

14) Which Nottingham Forest midfield player was bought in January 2017?
Henri Lansbury

15) Which central midfielder was sold to Everton in August 2016?
Idrissa Gueye

16) Defender Christopher Samba signed on a free from where in July 2017?
Panathinaikos

17) Which two players were sold to Fiorentina in the summer of 2017?
Carlos Sanchez and Jordan Veretout

18) From where was John McGinn signed in August 2018?
Hibernian

19) Who was bought from Club Brugge in June 2019?
Wesley

20) Which player left to join Deportivo in July 2018?
Carles Gil

21) Which defender was bought from Southampton in July 2019?
Matt Targett

22) Who was brought in from Manchester City in July 2019?
Douglas Luiz

23) Which player was purchased from Genk in the 2020 January transfer window?
Mbwana Samatta

24) From which Italian club was Pepe Reina loaned in January 2020?
AC Milan

Cup Games – Answers

1) Who scored the only goal of the game as Chelsea beat Aston Villa 1-0 in the FA Cup Final in 2000?
Roberto Di Matteo

2) Which club knocked Villa out in the Europa League Qualifying Rounds in both 2009 and 2010?
Rapid Vienna

3) Who put Villa 1-0 up in the 2010 League Cup Final, before they eventually lost 2-1 to Manchester United?
James Milner

4) Which Manchester United player controversially avoided a red card for his foul on Gabby Agbonlahor inside the first 5 minutes of that final?
Nemanja Vidic

5) Villa beat Ajax 2-1 in the Group Stage of the UEFA Cup in 2008 thanks to goal from which two players?
Martin Laursen and Gareth Barry

6) Aston Villa were knocked out of the League Cup in the Second Round in 2018 by which side?
Burton Albion

7) Which team did Villa beat 8-3 away from home in the League Cup Second Round in 2005?
Wycombe Wanderers

8) Which Croatian team knocked Aston Villa out of the UEFA Cup in the First Round in 2001?
NK Varazdin

9) Who scored the winner in the last minute of extra time to secure a 3-2 win over Leicester City in the League Cup Third Round in October 2006?
Gabby Agbonlahor

10) Who knocked Villa out of the FA Cup at the Third Round stage in 2018?
Peterborough

11) Villa reached the League Cup Final by beating Blackburn Rovers in the Semi Final Stage in 2010, but what was the remarkable score in the second leg?
Aston Villa 6-4 Blackburn Rovers

12) Who scored the winner as Aston Villa beat Liverpool 2-1 in the 2015 FA Cup Semi Final?
Fabian Delph

13) What was the final score as Arsenal beat Villa in the 2015 FA Cup Final?
4-0

14) Which lower league team beat Villa over two legs in the 2013 League Cup Semi Final?
Bradford City

15) Who scored the Aston Villa goal as they lost the 2020 League Cup Final 2-1 to Manchester City?
Mbwana Samatta

First Goals II – Answers

1) Stiliyan Petrov
   Sheffield United

2) Christian Benteke
   Swansea City

3) Milan Baros
   Blackburn Rovers

4) Mbwana Samatta
   Bournemouth

5) Kevin Phillips
   Bolton Wanderers

6) Darren Bent
   Manchester City

7) Barry Bannan
   Rapid Vienna

8) Ciaran Clark
   Arsenal

9) Rudy Gestede
   Bournemouth

10) Lewis Grabban
    Preston North End

11) John Terry
    Fulham

12) Jack Grealish
    Leicester City

13) John McGinn
    Sheffield Wednesday

14) Tyrone Mings
    Sheffield United